WINE PAIRING:

THE BASIC KNOWLEDGE NEEDED TO FEEL CONFIDENT PAIRING FOOD AND WINE

Erik Toröd

CONTENTS

1 INTRODUCTION

Thank you for purchasing this book, "Wine pairing: The basic knowledge needed to feel confident pairing food and wine"!

I am going to be honest from the start. There is no definite truth to what is a great combination of wine and food, because taste is subjective and everyone has different preferences. However, there are scientifically proven flavors whom are objectively the same for everyone. There are five of them and they are: sweetness, acidity, saltiness, bitterness and umami. These flavors can be measured and everyone will agree on the results, for example that sugar is sweet and lime juice is acidic.

They all react with each other differently and the key to wine pairing is to understand how they affect one another in the combination of food and wine. As I previously said taste is subjective and everyone is different, but there is still a general opinion of what people like and dislike that is very similar for everyone. Following that will greatly increase the chances that everyone at the dinner will appreciate the wine and food pairing.

You should not put it on yourself to memorize everything in this book right away. There are many small things to remember, but in time with a little trial and error you will know them all. If you ever feel uncertain when making a pairing, open up this book again and use it as a reference for your situation.

Now, we will start by looking closer at the separate effects of each flavor and some sensations in the mouth.

2 FLAVOURS

SWEETNESS

You can find sweetness in most ingredients and wines because sugar can exist in many different forms. Although every one of them have the same flavor, sweet.

The sweetness found in wine has several effects on the wine and food pairing. It will balance the sweetness in the food. That means that a sweet dish with a sweet wine will actually be experienced as less sweet together than separately. Wines that are not sweet are considered dry.

Sweetness in a dish, on the other hand, will as previously stated try to balance itself with the sweetness in the wine. In doing that, it will reduce the experience of sweetness and thereby make the wine drier as well as more acidic. It will also amplify the taste of bitterness which is generally considered a negative experience.

It is typically very hard to pair a dry wine with a dish containing some sweetness. Even if we tasted the wine before making the pairing and thought it had a balanced taste, an uneven balancing of sweetness in the pairing of food and wine will, in this case, make the wine taste even drier as well as amplify its acidity and bitterness.

Some examples of food high in sweetness would be fruits, vegetables like peas, carrots, corn as well as cheese, cream and ketchup.

ACIDITY

Acidity is a very important component of both food and wine, but we have to remember that almost every human being will react negatively to higher amounts of acidity since it historically has been a warning to us that the food we were eating had gone bad. Acidity is however very useful as it has a noticeable effect on all other flavors. Just like with sweetness, acidity in a dish will balance itself with the acidic content in a wine, and by doing that the sweetness will be amplified.

The acid in a dish will reduce a wine's bitterness and make it less dry (making it sweeter). It will also reduce the taste of umami and give red wines a smoother mouthfeel. This is generally considered a good thing as it gives more room to the other flavors in a dish as well as increases the taste of fruitiness in the wine.

You can think of acid and sweetness in these situations as countermeasures to each other. If the sweetness increases the acidity is reduced, and if acidity is increased sweetness is reduced. This also goes the other way around, although it is generally harder to remove ingredients than it is to add more.

Almost every wine contains high amounts of acid, so making sure there is something acidic in the dish will help create a balance. We remember that sweetness reduces acidity, but what would happen if we tried to pair a dry acidic wine with a very sweet food? The sweetness found in the dish will not be able to create a balance with a dry wine and will almost completely remove the sweet flavor from it. This will make the wine taste even more acidic and the pairing would be almost undrinkable. If a dish for some reason cannot contain acidity, make sure to buy a wine with little acidity to prevent this from happening.

A lot of people have a hard time with very dry red wines. Make sure that if you should buy one of those there is some kind of acid available to reduce it, maybe as a small side dish. Something as simple as a slice of lemon to squeeze on the food would make a huge difference for those people, making a pairing that they normally would hate to something they most likely will enjoy!

Examples of food that has a high acidic content would be citrus fruits, pickled vegetables, yogurt, Crème Fraiche and mustard.

But what about ingredients that have both acidity and sweetness? For example, tropical fruits, chutneys and tomato sauce? In those cases, we will have to taste them and see whether it is sweetness or acidity that is dominant. Depending on the answer the reaction between the food and wine in the pairing will be different. If the dish is more acidic than the wine, the wine is going to be experienced as sweeter, fruitier and less acidic. However, that increased sweetness will also give the wine a rougher mouthfeel. If it is the other way around and the dish is sweeter than the wine, the wine will be experienced as dry, acidic and not very fruity at all.

Do not feel disheartened about the consequences of failing to create a balance. It is hard, but as long as we are close to a balance the pairing will still work nicely and you will most likely still get compliments, it is just not going to be as great.

BITTERNESS

You probably remember that lingering unpleasant taste you have after drinking too much coffee, that is bitterness. You can learn to appreciate bitterness, but it is believed that we are genetically created to be cautious of it because in the past food that had a bitter taste was most likely poisonous. Therefore, it will not require a lot of bitterness to make a person politely take a few sips and then leave their wine at a dinner party when a pairing has been made that is very bitter.

It is easy to believe that since sweetness is balanced by sweetness, and acidity is balanced by acidity in a pairing, the same would go for bitterness. That is not the case, pairing a bitter dish with a bitter wine will amplify the bitter taste in both.

Red wines will in almost every case have more bitterness in them when compared to white wines. This is because of how they are made. White wines are made from the juice of the grape while red wines are made from the juice, pulp and skin, and they contain something called tannic acid. Without going deep into chemical reactions, tannic acids react with our mucosa and by doing that is making us more sensitive to bitterness. Therefore, it is generally a good idea to pair a white wine with a food containing bitter ingredients. An example of a dish with a lot of bitterness would be a salad.

The bitter taste in both wine and food is reduced by acidity, and further reduced when the acidity is combined with salt. Bitterness is however amplified by sweetness, umami and bitterness which is important to remember as making a mistake here is one of few things that can actually ruin a pairing.

Some examples of ingredients with a lot of bitterness would be arugula, endives, grapes, cacao and bell peppers.

SALTINESS

Salt is extremely important when cooking and we add it to almost every dish to enhance the ingredients own flavor. It is important to remember that salt is easy to overuse, which can ruin an entire dish, so add it in small increments. An even better thing to do would be to use some salt and then let everyone at the dinner table add more if they desire.

Examples of ingredients containing salt would be cured meats, seafood, soy, cheese and olives. If one of these ingredients or any other ingredient containing high amounts of salt is a part of a dish, you need to consider it when making a wine pairing, even if there is very little of them.

There are only a few wines in the world that actually contain salt but there are a few exceptions. Those wines are made from grapes that have grown in coastal areas in soil rich in sea salt. However, they do not contain enough salt to play a noticeable part while making a wine pairing, so we will from now on assume that all wines are free from salt.

Salt in a dish will reduce the taste of acidity, and

together with acidity it will reduce bitterness and give the wine a smoother mouthfeel. Together that will make the wine taste fruitier.

If you were to make a dish containing high amounts of salt, make sure to pair it with a very acidic wine, as the salt will reduce the acidity and make the wine taste fruitier and sweeter. A wine with little acidity to a salty food would most likely become way too sweet for most people's liking.

When using a flavored salt, make sure to consider the tasting properties of the ingredient flavoring the salt.

UMAMI

Umami is the fifth flavor and although it has been known for hundreds of years in most Asian countries, it was not scientifically isolated until the 20:th century, which is why it is not as known in most western countries. It has a very delicate flavor and is easily hidden behind the other more dominant ones. However, it has a very big effect on wine, and therefore it is very useful to know what ingredients that contains a high concentration of it.

When umami meets wine, it tends to make the wine taste stronger, more bitter and in some cases giving it what could best be described as a metallic aftertaste which is not very pleasant. When umami is paired with a red wine it will also give the wine a rougher mouthfeel and amplify its bitterness further. Thankfully the effects of umami can be reduced by acidity and salt.

Umami is actually in most ingredients which are further increasing the importance of acidity and salt in the dish every time we make a food and wine pairing. However, the highest concentration of it is found in the following ingredients: Fish containing high amounts of fat, like tuna and salmon. All seafood, aged hard cheese and soy. Eggs have a very troublesome level of umami which makes it very hard, but doable to pair dishes such as an omelet with wine. Vegetables also contain high concentrations of umami.

With vegetables and fruits, the amount of umami increases as it ripens, but as it starts to overripe the umami concentration will start to decline again. That is why we find fruits and vegetables to taste the best when they are at their peak of ripeness.

The easiest way to handle umami is to make sure every ingredient is properly salted and acidic when possible. The more ingredients with high concentrations of umami, like vegetables, the further we should move from red wines with dry mouth feels and more towards smooth white wines. Even if you would find these pairings balanced, taste is subjective so other people may be more sensitive and will therefore have a harder time to appreciate the pairings where high umami ingredients are present. A great tip when pairing wine with a dish high in umami is therefore to have a lemon wedge on the side that people can squeeze on top of the food to reduce the experienced effect of umami, if necessary.

3 SENSATIONS

Red wines (and a few white wines) contain tannins and they are responsible for causing the dry and rough mouthfeel we sometimes get when drinking. Instead of going into detail about the chemical reactions they cause and are a part of, we will just remember this: More tannins result in a drier and rougher mouthfeel.

The dry sensation caused by tannins is amplified by sweetness, umami, bitterness and spiciness. Therefore, it is generally a good idea to make sure every dish contains some acid and salt to reduce it. Fat and food with creamy consistencies will also help smoothen the rough mouth feeling.

Red wines will always contain a higher amount of tannins compared to white wines because of how they are made. A white wine is made from the juice of a grape, but a red is made from the juice, pulp and skin, and that is where we can find most tannins. Few people mind the dry mouthfeel from red wines alone, but in a pairing with a dish that lacks proper salting and acidity it can quickly become unpleasant. Always keep this in mind when pairing red wines with those kinds of dishes.

An easy way to reduce the risk of people finding the pairing unpleasant is to have some kind of sauce with the dish based on something acidic like wine, vinegar or something creamy. You can experience the huge difference this makes for yourself. Go out and buy a dry red wine and make something with a lot of umami, a steak for example. Also, make a sauce. Take a bite of the steak first and then take a sip of the wine, it will not be very pleasant. After that, eat some more of it together with the sauce and the taste of the wine will be a lot better. I promise.

Another important thing to remember is that we can adapt and get used to this dry sensation which means that if you drink a lot of dry wine yourself and find a pairing balanced, your guests or family may not since you have an easier time with the rough mouthfeel. A rule of thumb I use is to always be safe and aim for a smoother mouthfeel than I personally find necessary.

HEAT AND SPICINESS

Spiciness is actually not a flavor, but a physical sensation created when spicy food reacts with our mucosa, almost causing a feeling of numbness. I keep coming back to the same statement, taste is subjective, especially when it comes to heat. Some people love it and others cannot stand it. The wine pairing can both amplify and reduce the sensation of spiciness in food, it depends on your choice. A wine with a high concentration of acid will reduce the sensation of heat and a wine with little acidity and a lot of sweetness will have an opposite effect.

Since spicy food will react with our mucosa and thereby make us even more sensitive to bitterness causing red wines to have an even rougher mouthfeel, which is generally not considered a good thing. Therefore, it is not a good idea to pair red wine with spicy food (although there are some exceptions). Instead go for a white wine with a lot of, or very little acidity depending on what you like. However, make sure that the wine is very fruity as it will almost pale in comparison to the spiciness if not.

FAT AND CREAMY CONSISTENCIES

While phenols and spiciness increase the mucosal sensitivity to bitterness and roughness, fat and creamy consistencies do the exact opposite. Making the wine taste smoother and less bitter. We do not need big amounts of fat to get the effect we wish, a little goes a long way. Common things that have this effect would be creamy sauces, stews, gratins and cheese so if you know you are drinking a rough red wine, try to include one of those in the meal.

If you are afraid the amount of fat in a dish will taste unpleasant to the people eating, add some acidity. It will not remove any fat, but it will make the eater experience the food as if it was much less fat than it actually is.

COOKING METHOD

Cooking an ingredient generally changes the taste of it. A good example of this would be a raw mushroom which raw is both bitter and has a high umami content. Basically, the worst thing to pair wine with. However, cooking it reduces the bitterness and umami as well as making it taste sweeter. All raw food are so-called wine foes making them a lot harder to pair with wine. If you still want to drink wine while eating something raw, I would suggest a smooth sweet wine with a high intensity, but with as little bitterness as possible. Most likely it will be a white one.

WINE FOES

There are some types of food that have a very negative effect on the taste of wine by bringing forward a metallic aftertaste. This includes almost all raw food, like vegetables, fruits, meats and fish with raw tomatoes and onions being some of the worst foes. Too much salt can also have this effect.

The easiest thing to do about this would be to just cook the food, for example, caramelized onions are incredible with any wine. However, adding something like a sauce with a fat and creamy consistency, or maybe a vinaigrette could compliment it. Just make sure that whatever you are adding to the dish works as a compliment to the ingredient causing problems.

4 PICKING A WINE TO PAIR WITH A DISH

Before buying the wine that will pair up nicely with our dish, there are a few things we need to consider.

- What ingredients are used in the dish?
- What are the tasting properties of those ingredients?
- How are we cooking the ingredients?
- How do the ingredients affect each other?
- What consistency will the food have when it is done?

After answering those questions, we should have a general idea of what type of wine to choose that will work nicely. However, if the unlikely situation would arise where there are no wines available that would work, we need to ask ourselves another question.

- Can I take any of the other wines available and maybe change the dish slightly?

If the answer to that question is yes, this is what we can do to the dish based on the previous sections of this book.

- Adding another side dish or changing the consistency of the ingredients so that it fits nicely with the wine.

- Removing a side dish with ingredients that do not fit together nicely with the wine.

- Removing or change the cooking method for one of the wine foes.

EXAMPLES:

STEAK WITH SAUTÉED MUSHROOMS AND POTATOES

We know that this dish contains high amounts of umami, fat and sweetness from the caramelization of the steak and the sautéed mushrooms. The rarer the steak is cooked; the less caramelization happens which reduces the need for sweetness in the wine. Umami makes wine taste more bitter, gives it a rougher mouthfeel and increases sweetness if not complemented by the sweetness in the wine.

Therefore, we now know that we need a wine with some sweetness to compensate. However, we will still have a problem with bitterness. What can we change? The easiest thing to do would be to add a fat or creamy consistency. For example, a sauce or maybe making mashed potatoes to compensate for the increased sensation of bitterness.

A Cabernet Sauvignon would be a nice pairing as its acidic content will help with the umami and fat, and its sweetness will balance nicely with the dish.

CRÈME BRULÉE WITH A BERRY COMPOTE

This dish contains high amounts of sweetness, as well as some acidity and a little bit of bitterness from the berries. However, since the Crème Brulée is creamy in itself, it will compensate for the bitterness of the berries without us doing anything. This leaves us with a dish that contains lots of sweetness and acidity. Therefore, we now know that we need a sweet wine to balance the sweetness of the food, but the wine also needs to contain acidity to balance out the berries acidity. A nice pairing to this would be a sweeter Muscat.

5 CHOOSING A DISH THAT COMPLEMENTS A WINE

On the other hand, maybe you have a bottle of wine at home already, but you don't know what food to pair with it. Try asking yourself the following questions.

- What are the tasting properties of my wine?

- What type of food would work with this wine's properties?

- What are the side dishes that could fit nicely with this wine?

When the dish is ready, taste it. Does it taste like you thought, or do you need to add anything, for example, acid, salt or sweetness? If the food is too bitter, then you could make a creamy sauce or add some cheese.

EXAMPLES

As for these examples, I will be using some of the bottles I already had at home but the same principles will apply to any wine.

CORRALILLO (WHITE ACIDIC WINE WITH MEDIUM BODY AND VERY LITTLE SWEETNESS)

Looking at the properties of this wine we can tell right away that the dish we are making should preferably not contain high amounts of sweetness, as the wine lacks the sweetness needed to balance it. As it is a medium-bodied wine a dish containing a lot of heat or fat would not be a great match either, but at the same time, it should not be completely free from them either. The dish will need acid to balance the acidity in the wine.

Because of that, I would suggest making fish or seafood because it is not very fatty, but at the same time not as lean as white meat. Both fish and seafood work well with acidity so squeezing some lemon juice on the dish would be an improvement and complement the wines own acidity nicely.

SIRO FIFTY (HIGH-BODIED RED WINE WITH A LOT OF ACID, LITTLE SWEETNESS AND A ROUGH MOUTHFEEL)

By looking at the properties of this wine we know that we will need a lot of flavors, either from fat or spices to complement the body of the wine. It also needs to be acidic but contain very little sweetness. Spicy food would not be optimal to pair with this wine as spicy dishes normally (not always) contain some sweetness to complement the heat which would amplify the rough mouth feeling. That leaves us with some food with a lot of flavor from fat. Beef, mushrooms or lamb would work. The wine is very acidic, so adding either salt or marinating the chosen ingredient in acid would tone down and balance the wine's acidity.

If you are like me and strongly prefer a smoother mouthfeel over a rough one, I would also make some kind of sauce to add some creaminess. Although the fat from the meat and the acid (if you decided to add acid to the dish) already does smoothen out the mouthfeel. However, this is just my preference. Experiment yourself and see what kind of mouthfeel you prefer.

6 SOMETHING WENT WRONG, HOW DO I FIX IT?

Unfortunately, every wine and food pairing we make will not be a great match. To hopefully help correct whatever problem arises, here comes some common issues and their corresponding solutions.

THE WINE IS TOO BITTER

When the wine in a pairing is too bitter for our preferences it is normally because the dish is too sweet and does not contain enough acid for the wine. To solve this, add some kind of acidity to the dish, like squeezing some lemon juice on it or add some acidity to the sauce by adding some vinegar or wine to it. Adding some fat, salt or something with a creamy consistency will also do the trick, like a Crème Fraiche or sour cream sauce.

If you feel none of these suggested solutions work in your situation, getting a new wine with less sweetness will make a better pairing.

THE WINE IS TOO ROUGH

The rough mouthfeel is caused by too much of either bitterness, spiciness or sweetness in the dish, which has amplified the wines roughness. In this case we can make two additions. Either add some salt and acidity together into the dish, or we can make the sauce creamier. If possible, we could also remove some sweetness in the dish, but that would require that the sweetness is found in a side dish.

In a situation where none of these alternatives would work for the dish, switching out the current wine for a smoother would be the way to go.

THE WINE IS TOO SWEET

This means that the wine did not have enough acidity to balance the acidity in the dish, and thereby amplifying the wines sweetness. Either add some acidity or see if you can remove one of the sweeter side dishes. Your current wine could also be replaced by a wine with a higher acidic content.

THE WINE IS TOO SOUR

In this case, the dish was too sweet for the wine, which means that the wines own sweetness was removed when balanced with the dish. Although it is not always possible, see if you could add some sweetness to the dish to help create a better balance. If the dish would not benefit from sweetness which normally is the case, you need to get a new wine with less sweetness and more acidity.

THE WINE GOT AN UNPLEASANT METALLIC AFTERTASTE

This is normally caused when a rough red wine is paired with ingredients high in umami. You can try to add a little bit of lemon juice or vinegar together with salt, but if that does not work you should see if you have a smoother red wine or a white wine to use instead.

THE WINE IS TASTELESS

This happens when you pair a flavor intensive dish with a fine and elegant wine, or if you previously had a wine with a high intensity. There are no alterations you can make to this pairing to fix it, just put the bottle aside for later and get a wine with a higher intensity.

7 GENERAL GUIDELINES AND SUMMARY

Although taste is subjective and everyone have different preferences when it comes to a food and wine pairing, there are common pairings that a clear majority of people enjoy. The following list is a short repetition of all the previous chapters, and following these guidelines will increase the chances that a pairing is appreciated.

- Food with acid needs a wine with acid.

- A wine with a high amount of tannins is best paired with food that contains a lot of fat or is very creamy.

- A sweet dish needs a sweet wine.

- If a dish contains several different flavors, make the pairing based on the most dominant one.

- Spicy food is best matched with a white wine low in tannins (not very bitter) that isn't very sweet. A Riesling is generally be a great pairing.

- If the food you are eating with the wine is too spicy, get a new wine with more acid.

- Vegetables, lighter fishes and carbohydrates are best with sparkling acidic white wines. A wine with these properties would be a Cava or Sauvignon Blanc.

- White meats, roasted vegetables and fish with a richer flavor is best paired with a white wine that also contains a little sweetness like Chenin Blanc or Riesling. Those wines also work great with vegetables, lighter fishes and carbohydrates.

- Tapas types of meals that contains many different flavors could be paired with either Chenin Blanc, Riesling or a lighter red like Pinot Noir. However, in this case you should consider the different ingredients tasting properties before going out and buying one of them.

- Medium bodied red wines like Merlot makes a good pairing with red meat.

- Red meats, as well as cured and smoked meats is also a good pairing with full bodied red wines, like a Cabernet Sauvignon.

This list is here to help you, but I would advise to not follow it blindly. Taking an extra 2-3 minutes and thinking about all the ingredients in your dish and how they will pair up with these wines could make a huge difference.

CONCLUSION

Thank you again for purchasing this book!

I hope it was able to help you build up more confidence with wine pairing because as you now have seen, it is not very hard. There are just a few things to remember. I would now suggest making a few food and wine pairings yourself and see how they end up, using the previous chapter to fix any pairings that did not come out great.

Your next step would be to try different pairings and see what you prefer. Maybe you like to have a high amount of acidity, or maybe you like the taste of bitterness. There is no right or wrong! You just need to figure out what works for you and your loved ones.

I would like to end this book with a special thank you to my friend André Lindh for all the help proofreading this book.

Thank you and good luck with your future pairings!

Erik Toröd

Printed in the USA
CPSIA information can be obtained
at www.ICGtesting.com
LVHW051037080224
771325LV00017B/117